Beers From The Pub, Served at Home

REVISED EDITION

ILLUSTRATED

© Max Barrington

I once met an old Gentleman in a bar who told me of this small poem, he may, or may not, have been the Author.

I have a few good reasons for drinking
And one of them just came into my head
If, a man can't drink, while he's living
Then, how the hell, can he drink when he's dead.

Max Barrington
Cairns City, Far North Queensland
AUSTRALIA

My story about how I became a 'Home Brewer' and of the failures and disasters that I experienced from the start.

It goes on to tell of my discovery into Pressure Brewing and kegging and how I have adopted this method with minimal equipment costs and have applied it to my 'Home Brewing'. The amount of money that I have saved is staggering, but the best part is that I have a beer that is second to none, it is just like to beer you would get at the pub, only better!

This New Edition book is now fully Illustrated for step by step beer brewing, and gear cleaning, so simple you will wonder why you didn't do this before

I was inspired to write this book, from the same person who inspired me to continue in my beer brewing challenge after many failures and disappointments, My darling Wife Lynette

Table of Contents

Before you get too excited
9

About This Book
11

A New Beginning
31

Back To The Drawing Board
40

What Gear Do You Need
46

Cleaning Your Gear
60

Where to brew
74

Let's do it
76

Kegging
116

BEFORE YOU GET TOO EXCITED

This is all about how you can brew your beer and then keg it to drink. It is not about bottling your beer, although, it can be Kegged and then bottled if you should want to for some reason, maybe going to a party, or whatever.

To make this happen, you will need to make a capital investment of around $2,000 (at the time of publication) this is for all new equipment, not second hand.

This equipment will be enough to produce 114 litres of beer each month, for a cost of approximately $160.

114 litres is the equivalent of 12 cartons of 24 x 360ml stubbies, which would retail for approximately, $660.

Of course, you don't have to produce 12 cartons each month, it's up to you, more if you like. At 12 cartons a month, you will be saving $500, each month, four months to replace your capital investment.

To make the Beer, you have to buy the Gear!

About This Book

I do know, that many people purchase a beer brewing extract kit in an attempt to brew beer for some reason or other, maybe to cut down on drinking costs and make your beer drinking more affordable, or maybe because the neighbour brews beer, or perhaps just a hobby?

There are though many who never attempt a second, or third brew and their equipment is laid to storage, or completely discarded, due to failure, or just too much effort to make it worthwhile.

This book may just make those people change their minds about home brewing beer.
For more advanced brewers, experts even, if you learn one new thing or pick up one new trick, then this book is well worth the small price you paid for it.

The brewing (How to Brew) instructions on the can of home brew beer extracts are so simple, so easy.

One set of instructions in particular, that is printed on the can of a very respected brand, has only about 240 words in 4 paragraphs consisting of 1 Mixing, 2 Fermenting, 3 Bottling, 4 Maturing. All in 240 (or thereabouts) words and also states to 'Add only sugar and water'. Simple, and it really is simple.....sort of.

Of course it is a sales ploy, because, if they add too much info, then it may turn potential new brewers away from purchasing this product.

It's not a scam! It's a great product, and most first time brews are successful, very successful in fact and even subsequent brews for that matter.

But, the issue could be, if you are considering home brewing with the view of never buying your usual supply of beer from the bottle shop again, but rely solely on your home brew, then do your calculations first on your required quantities and the time involved to do this.

In most cases, it will not work for you.

Why, well most people buy a kit with a 23 litre fermenter and 30 PET bottles included plus a 1.7 litre can of extract with the yeast under the top. It most probably also has a 1kg pack of booster or, a dextrose/sugar pack.

They follow all the instructions through to bottling, which, takes around two weeks, then following another two weeks for the second ferment in the bottles, comes the tasting. It has taken four weeks to come to this point where you get to taste your brew.

It tastes great, so what's the problem?

The problem may be that, thirty bottles of 750ml beer will only last until another batch is ready if you drink only one bottle each day.

So…..if your usual consumption is around a six pack of 375ml stubbies a day, then in theory, you're going to need three 23 litre fermenters and ninety 750ml bottles and do three brews a month.

A lot of work! Washing and sterilising fermenters and bottles. Hmmmmm.

This is where a lot of people become disillusioned with brewing their own beer, just too much work, not to mention, all the gear you need, and the space to keep it.

But! If you do it my way, IT WILL WORK (well, it should work) and you will save heaps of dollars, not only brewing it yourself but also enjoying the taste and the convenience of not having to visit the bottle shop and drag heavy cartons of beer home.

I am not an expert in the home brewing of beer or any other brewing, for that matter, and may be judged, by brewing experts to be totally incorrect with respect to my methods of home brewing beer, kegging beer and cleaning/sanitising of my equipment.

Some brewers will be in total disagreement, whilst others may be enlightened, of that I am sure, as I really think that many brewers have acquired a taste for their own brews, and believe them to be the best, as it is the best they can achieve.

But, the methods I use are simple, and they require very little effort. They are cost effective and, certainly work for me.

I would also mention that with my present system of beer brewing, I have produced over 2,280 litres of rather excellent home brew beer within the last twelve months. Surprised? That is only 120 x 19 L kegs, or 13 schooners of beer for every day of the week and I don't drink it all on my own, we get lots of visitors.

As I said, I am not an expert in brewing, nor a connoisseur of beers. This book is entirely the result of peer pressure from my darling wife and fellow beer drinkers, relatives, friends and neighbours who have tasted and drank my final method/recipe beer.

I know very little with respect to beer brewing terminology and technology, or it's chemistry and only a little when it comes to physics. I do, however, know how to analyse systems or ideas and do basic research to make things happen, not to mention some logistics. I am sadly, not a wealthy person who is able to splash out on expensive equipment, I was however very surprised by the amount of money I have saved in a short time by producing my own beer. I am talking in the thousands of dollars, truly.

I am just a person who decided to brew my own beer at home, but, I wanted a beer at least as good as, or better, than I could buy. The same beer, or better, that I would be served in a pub or club, the same beer, or better, that I would buy at a bottle shop, I mean like, if you can't brew at least that good, why bother.

I did not want to create a great effort, expense or requirement for home space that I don't have living in a two bedroom unit, nor did I want a 'Home Brew' taste like cardboard or a cloudy beer and I did not want a beer in a bottle with a residual at the bottom of it, and believe me, I was told by some quite experienced home brewers, **that what I wanted, was not possible** and I would never achieve as good as 'commercial' beer, but I would, after time, **acquire a taste** for homebrew and would believe it to be as good as but in most cases, much better. No Way!

I did not want to have to acquire a taste for home brewed beer, I certainly didn't want a beer that I would have to tell friends that it gets better the more you drink! Nor did I want a beer that people would refuse a second drink.

I was convinced that I could, in fact, produce my own beer, that I or my family and friends, could enjoy that, as mentioned previously, tasted just like the beer they normally buy from pubs, clubs and bottle shops.

This book will tell of my failures upon commencing my first and subsequent brews, which got better or worse and how, through my research, I came to the point, where my brew, has achieved my ultimate goal, to the stage where I am happy with what I am producing and no longer, do I attempt any changes, I have no reason to do so.

This book will detail everything, that is required to produce a remarkable beer that most will enjoy, including how to make slight differences for particular tastes.

It explains in detail the all equipment I use, where to source from and approximate costs as per the date of this publication, and goes on to explain the methods I use for easily cleaning of equipment, what recipe I use and the method. How my brewing takes place and finally how I keg the beer.

If you are also wondering how I drink beer, I have included how to choose beer glasses and most important, how to clean them in order to retain a head.

It takes me around 3.5 hours to put on a brew and keg it including all cleaning. That's 57 litres.

It Begins

I love beer and so does my wife, not to mention our grown up children, we drink glass Stubbies at home and once drank schooners in pubs and clubs until my wife was served a drink with, what we think was a drug, at a venue in Melbourne in her drink.

Following that, we commenced to drink only Stubbies in pubs and clubs, which is a bit dumb when you think about it, as you can drink a Stubby at home for a fraction of the price.

We finally got to retire and continued to enjoy our 'xxxx gold stubbies' but now we weren't working we couldn't see any sense in waiting till around 6 pm to have a beer.

So our beer consumption went up from around, 3~4 stubbies each to around, 5~ 6 stubbies each per day, not hard to do, believe me. That's from about two cartons of 24 stubbies each week to around four cartons.

The price of gold stubbies back then was around $42 per carton, which gets the beer bill each week in the vicinity of $168, and if you look at that annually, it's a staggering $8736. And that is most likely very conservative, due to family and friends visiting, so the annual bar bill is more likely to balance around the $10,000 mark.

If that price amazes you and sounds unbelievable, take a minute to calculate how much you spend on *your* beer each year. I did not add any visits to the pubs and/or clubs in that period, just too scary.

I mentioned earlier, that I had brewed 2,280 litres of beer within the last 12 months, sounds like a lot? If you convert it back to cartons of 24 stubbies it works out around 4 cartons per week, and that would supply my wife and myself plus about, one, or two cartons a week for visitors and the occasional party throughout the entire year. And when you look at it that way it's not excessive in my way of thinking, we drink nothing other than beer and water, so we don't spend money on any type of spirits. And as Slim would say "we never ever, ever, get rolling drunk"

Incidentally, the cost of the 2280 litres of beer that I brewed cost me around $2964 not including, one time, capital expenditure of equipment. Converted to cost of equivalent, 240 x 24 stubby cartons at $42 from the bottle shop $10,080, that's what I estimated earlier. That gives me a saving of $7,116 per year,... suits me!

Anyhow, we enjoyed our stubbies in our 'al fresco' dining area next to our pool, now known as 'the beer garden', and in fact installed a refrigerator in this area to make life even easier.

Visitors were always welcome to our home, and from time to time, our children, and grandchildren, who all lived either interstate or a great distance, would visit on occasions and also seemed to enjoy 'the beer garden'.

We had neighbours around one Sunday afternoon, and they brought with them, some bottles of their home brew, which we placed into the refrigerator and served them a stubby of Gold.

After we drank the Gold, one of the neighbours retrieved some of the home brews from the fridge and I found some glasses. I was at first reluctant to try this homebrew, from previous encounters of homebrew, and was rather wishing the neighbours had not brought it with them, but I did not want to refuse as it may have offended them.

As mentioned earlier, I had in the past tasted homebrew from others, with sad results. It always seemed to have an off' taste which caused me to refuse a second drink. I think this taste is referred to as 'home brew', or cardboard taste and has always left me thinking, how on earth can people enjoy such a drink, impossible, but as one home brewer said to me that he felt morally obliged to drink it, now that he had paid for it and made it, as his wife would crucify him if he did not. But, he said, it gets better after a few! ....Not for me, no way.

I think another thing that turned me off, was the environment in which the beer was brewed, in most instances the shed with all the condiments like oil grease, wood shavings, sawdust, garden chemicals and rat sack or the garage with diesel or petrol fumes, or, simply the backyard, yuk!

On this day I gingerly tasted my neighbour's home brew beer, which he had poured carefully into glasses, to avoid the residual that lay at the bottom of the PET bottle, although this made me shudder in anticipation, the beer looked quite clear.

I took a taste, and could not believe it, and took a second taste and then a good swig, wow how good was this, after the homebrew, I went back to the Gold Stubby and it did not seem as good as it was before tasting the homebrew. This homebrew was very clear with lots of working bubbles and a nice foamy head, on previous occasions of tasting home brew, the beer was cloudy and fairly flat looking, which certainly distracted me from the taste, so to me it was horrible.

But, this one was different, and I was interested and quizzed the neighbour on its production.

He went on to describe the process of his 25 litre fermenter and the sugar, the extract, the washing of the bottles, the sanitising of the bottles, the filling of the bottles and so on and so on, well before he had finished explaining I had lost total interest and opened another Goldie.

This neighbour was a baker by trade and was very meticulous in his measurements, methods and cleanliness.

He added that by the time he brewed 23 litres, leaving a little headspace, and bottled into 30 x 750ml PET bottles which was the equivalent to two and a half cartons of stubbies, it took at least twelve to fourteen days in the fermenter, then a further twelve to fourteen days of second fermentation and carbonation, which was about a month all up, equalling a bit over a stubby each, for both him and his wife a day, it did just did not work for him and it would be much, too much, effort to run two fermenters, so he only brewed beer on rare occasions as he had to buy beer from the bottle shop anyway. How sad!......why would you really bother? Even though it was a good drop.

I did ask him if he had thought of kegging. He said that he had considered kegging but had not looked into it as he thought it may have been too tricky and too expensive and the amount of beer he and his wife consumed probably did not warrant it.

I later thought that the neighbour's brew, though a very pleasant drop was certainly not worth the effort in my opinion, that he had revealed in the process of creating such a drink.

No way was I prepared to wait 28 odd days for a brew to be ready for drinking, it would mean that I would need at least four to five 24 litre, fermenters and countless bottles.

But, home brewed beer was in the back of my mind, and I found myself casually looking online with respect to home brewing and it was here that I found out about kegging, which to me seemed much less energetic than bottling, and possibly perfect for us, due to the quantity of beer both my wife and I consumed, not to mention visitors.

It was on Gumtree that I saw a home brew setup for sale consisting of a kegerator with a two tap font, 60 litre fermenter, 3 x 19 litre kegs, 1 x 2.4kg and a 3.5kg Co2 cylinders that were about 50% full and a fridge controller.

All for $750 seemed good to me so we drove down to Brisbane and bought the bundle.

The guy I bought it from said whatever I did, and however I brewed, to make sure everything was kept clean and sanitised. He went along to say that when empty, the kegs should be filled with a solution such as nappi san or similar, that contained sodium percarbonate as with the fermenter.

He was certainly practising what he preached as all the gear was still full of a nappi san solution and it really stank of it.

On the way home I called into the home brew shop in Maryborough.

I had a chat with the guy in the store and told him that I am a xxxx gold drinker and that I was about to start brewing and kegging.

He suggested I try Morgans Qld Gold with 500g of Body Blend and Cluster hops and to use the yeast under the lid.

I bought three of each as suggested to make up 60 litres along with some Morgans sanitiser.

That evening I watched about a dozen YouTube videos on home beer brewing and kegging. Some of the kegging that showed closed transfer was, I thought, out of my league and concentrated on gravity filling the kegs from a tube attached to the fermenter's tap.

The brewing itself looked easy enough and so I began by cleaning all the gear with a sodium per carbonate based cleaner as directed by the guy I bought the gear from and applying sanitiser to everything.

I had a beer fridge in the garage which I stripped the shelves, and the fermenter fitted perfectly but very close to the top of the inside of the fridge.

There was just enough room for the airlock and would not permit adding fluids by means of a jug. But! I had a problem, in fact, a couple of problems. How do I fill the fermenter with water, 60 litres of water weighs 60 kilos and at my age I could no longer lift that weight, I decided that the extract and blend mixture weighing around 10 kilos would go into the fermenter first while the fermenter was out of the fridge, then the fermenter would be placed into the fridge where water would be added by hose, simple.

The next issue was placing the brew, once completed, from the fermenter into the kegs, the tap of the fermenter whilst in the fridge was around 450mm from the ground and the top of the kegs was about 600mm.

That was not really an issue as the tubing to fit to the bottom of the keg from the tap was flexible, the main problem was I would run out of gravity to fill the third keg, which meant I would have to lift the fermenter from the fridge and place on a higher surface after filling two kegs, certainly not ideal, but so be it.

I then followed the instructions on the Morgans cans, mixed, and applied all ingredients to the fermenter. I fitted the temperature controller and set it at 25°C and waited in anticipation for the brew to be ready for kegging. The instructions said that complete fermentation should be in 5 days at 25°C and the specific gravity should read 1005 or lower.

After 5 days I took a sample by use of the fermenter's tap into a glass jug and, it did not look too appetising at all and, was very cloudy, but the smell was not unpleasant, the gravity reading I took seemed to be about 1015 which is way out from what the manufacturer recommends, hmmm, time to think, is it cloudy because the sample is from the bottom?

As with the SG reading, from the bottom of the fermenter,……..of course!…..so, it must be ready to keg.

The next (YouTube) instruction was, fridge down to 3°C, turn down the fridge controller to 3°C and left it till the next day.

It took two days (nights) to get the temperature controller's reading down to 3°C and I was disappointed to find a large block of ice within the brew, another lesson?

Filling the kegs was a lot easier than I had anticipated, even lifting the fermenter from the fridge to a higher surface to fill the last, 3rd keg. I could not tell whether the brew was clear or not whilst kegging but did appear to be "clearish".

I placed the lids on the kegs and applied 25 psi of Co_2 to each keg as per 'YouTube', then placed them into the kegerator and patiently waited for three days as advised by various kegging experts.

The day had arrived, I connected the Co2 at 7 psi to the inlet of the keg then connected the beer line to the kegs 'out' and here we go.

After allowing the froth to settle, a sip,......another sip, hmmm, wife takes a sip and I notice a strange look on her face, she takes another sip and looks at me and asks what I think, not bad I respond but in reality, it wasn't that good and I added that it is drinkable even if you can't see through it. I don't think she believed me.

In reality, this beer was not good, It, was not what I wanted. I was expecting exactly the same, as you would be served in a pub or club. I think I must have been very naive, on the Morgans can the beer looked a lot better than what we had here.

It did not look good and it did not taste good, it was drinkable and you could get used to it, but it was not what I wanted.

Two options are abort the idea of homebrew, or improve the brew and get it right.

The first option was not really an option as I had just invested around $900 and my time and it was really only a first try, which really only left one option, improve!

Whilst drinking our very first home brewed beer and trying to convince ourselves that it was in fact quite acceptable, but we both knew it wasn't. I was seeking more and more advice, which seemed to vary so much to the extent that it was so contradictory, that it was totally useless.

The guy over the road from where I lived, I had learned was in fact not only a home brewer, but also a kegger. The day that I approached him, with the view of seeking advice, he just happened to have, what I assumed to be, a glass of his home brew in his hand, which appeared to me more like a frothy tea with milk.

Sadly, I knew instantly that any advice from this source would be null and void.

The local brew shop was most helpful with suggestions such as improving the taste by removing the Cluster hops, filtering the water, and not using the yeast that comes with the brew (nobody uses it, don't know why they put it there) try this yeast instead at only $7.50 per pack, try adding finings to clear the brew, try different brand brews, brewing too hot and not long enough, make sure your SG readings are accurate. Not to mention, sell, sell, sell. Try this, try that.

Another culprit, the brew shop mentioned, and the most probable, was that it may be contamination from various things including 'Air'.

I had an invitation from a fellow brewer that I met at the brew shop, to come around and try my brew. I thought this may be a real chance to learn more about successful brewing and kegging and accepted the very kind offer only to find this fellow's brew was all foam, he first poured from the keg into a glass beer jug and "let It settle a minute" he said. It was flat and an even worse colour, and very bitter, than what I was producing, but he thought it was the best in the country. I made a suggestion that it was flat and he was mortified. I didn't stay for a second beer, even though he said it gets better after he had poured a few.

This caused me to realise that some people, do acquire a taste for their home brew, so of course they believe it to be better than beer from the pub and in reality, if it's what some people want, fair enough.

All good suggestions, which all cost money and time, as in brewing time and trying them, but try them all and much more I did with some better results and plenty of mistakes, but I soon realised that I had to *brew the beer for much longer than the manufacturer's instructions stated* if I wanted a better beer.

I also realised that by allowing longer, brewing times would not allow me to produce the quantities of beer that we required and we would also need to either cut down on drinking and that was *not going to happen*, or, also buy beer from the bottle shop. No Way!..

I bought another, 60 litre fermenter, a second hand refrigerator and another temperature controller, to allow for longer brewing times in the hope of improving clarity and taste.

I, also installed a small, 180 litre, water tank to collect rainwater, which I then filtered for brewing. This was to combat the very poor drinking water where we then lived and I was learning that water was a *very* important consideration.

I brewed every week from February to May a total of 16 brews trying out different brand brew extracts, varying dextrose measurements, adding corn syrup and malts, and trying different yeasts.

During this period we did have visitors from time to time and of course, neighbours also called in and I would pour them an 'on tap' beer which at first looked impressive until the head of the beer disappeared, and it was then noticed that the beer seemed a little, well maybe, very cloudy, and a funny smell, but! They all exclaimed it was a very nice drop, they didn't, however, accept a second beer. They were being polite, they did never once say "Max! This beer is shit", although I am sure, they thought it.

The result after additional expense and time was sad, to say the least, not much difference in improvement.

It still, was not what I wanted and it would never really replace our beloved XXXX Gold stubbies. It was in fact a real treat to go to the club and have a XXXX stubby, not good and very deflating.

It wasn't until I had to pour three kegs, into the drain out the back and replace the equivalent of six cartons of beer with XXXX Gold, at a cost of about $240 that we realised, just how good this XXXX Gold was to drink, and that maybe home brewing was just not for us and that our homebrew days, were coming to an end, and rapidly.

Indeed the home brewing days would have come to an end then and there, had it not been for the amount of money I had spent on this sad, failed project.

The guy I had bought the gear from in the first place, told me he was on a health kick and had stopped drinking, *lying prick*, I thought as I tried to imagine how I was going to sell this gear and just write the whole exercise off as a bad investment, end of the story, also to cut down on drinking as we just could no longer afford to keep drinking like it was 'going out of fashion', and within a short period of time, our beloved xxxx gold rose in price from 2 cartons for $80 to around $45 for each carton and threatening to increase even higher, not good as we loved drinking beer.

A NEW BEGINNING

I am a member of a Facebook Group called 'Home Brewing Australia', where I obtained heaps of advice from the other members, in relation to their personal brewing experiences, but mostly revolving around grain brewing rather than the manufactured cans of extracts, of which many seemed to put down as a quite inferior mode of home brewing.

As can be seen, if you visit this page, it mostly talks of grain brewing and grain brewing equipment, but it does however, show some pictures of finished glasses of beer and some look really appetising whilst others are rather less appetising and some are labelled, 'craft beer'.

Some time ago I visited a 'craft beer' brewery in Cairns with my wife and son. Looking at the large array of beers available we had no idea of what to order or try when it was suggested, by bar staff, that we each try a paddle.

This paddle is simply a small tray of six 100ml glasses of samples of selected premium craft beers available. Of the six beers on this paddle, we drank only one entirely, and that was the most clearest, looking beer, it was their most popular lager, and one 100ml glass was certainly enough, very strong raw sugar taste.

We merely took one sip of each of another four and left one completely alone due to appearance and odour. The guy at the Brewery told me, not to drink with my eyes, and I will enjoy it more, no way!....I then decided that craft beers were not for me. It was not just the look of it, all except one of those brews, tasted somewhat like my previous failures.

Interestingly, I had recently noticed, that a craft brewery had posted an expression of interest on Facebook, asking for comments with the view of hosting an 'Oktoberfest' at their premises. Most of the comments proffered were similar to, "Did you get onto some good beer?" or "Have you got Great Northern on". Plus, other similar remarks and quite a few snide remarks pertaining to beer quality. Craft beers are not, it seems for everyone.

I read somewhere, on the Facebook 'Home Brewing Australia' group page, that mentioned another group called 'Fermzilla Users – tips and recipes'. I had no idea what a Fermzilla is, but it is obviously connected to beer brewing, so I found and also joined this Facebook group.

To say I was really amazed at what I found within this group would be an understatement. The members on this page spoke of pressure fermentation, a new way of fermenting that helped eliminate yeast, and other types of infections, as well as carbonating the brew as it ferments.

One, Fermzilla Users feed went on to say that,

Pressure fermenting is becoming a hot topic among beer communities with both micro and macro breweries now using pressure fermentation. In traditional gravity fermentation, CO_2 from the fermenting beer is allowed to escape, and whilst a simple process a transfer is required from the primary fermentation to the secondary fermentation in bottles or kegs to allow for carbonation. This transfer process allows for air contamination, which is far from ideal, whilst with pressure fermentation the fermenter is sealed and the CO_2 is held inside the fermenter to allow carbonation within the same vessel.

'Air contamination' jumped out at me, the guys at the brew store had mentioned this.

Also allows for 'closed transfer' to kegs to eliminate any further chance of air contamination.

Sounds good to me, and somewhere in this Facebook group, was mention of yet still another Facebook group, called 'KegLand home brew community'.

So I decided to also join that group to extend my journey into this pressure brewing.

And, that group, led me to discover the website, 'KegLand', who actually manufacture and retails, amongst thousands of other brewing items, the 60 litre Fermzilla for around $80 ex Noble Park Vic. Sounds good I thought well, let's investigate.

I read everything I could find about Fermzilla, and I watched on, YouTube, how the Fermzilla actually worked, I was convinced that pressure brewing was well worth a try and seemed, a fairly low cost experiment to get into it.

A big problem was the freight from Noble Park to Cairns was around $200, on top of the price for two Fermzilla's, $400 in total, plus all the ancillary gear I would need might just sway my financial manager (wife) away from this idea, but, as fate would have it we were heading off on a road trip to visit the daughter in Tassie in a few weeks, and I could make these Fermzilla's fit neatly into the back of our Subaru Outback quite easily, and save $200 plus the freight cost of other items I required.

This sales pitch worked excellently and it was agreed to purchase a pair of Fermzilla's and sell the current two 60 litre fermenters, if we could. As it was, we ended up giving these to my brother in law who makes tomato sauce (well each to his own I guess).

If you have not yet done so, check out the KegLand website. I thought It must be the very first stop for brewing equipment and excellent value. Just so sad that we are so far from Noble Park.

I ordered two 60 litre Fermzilla all rounders and all the gear, I thought, that I required, on line and arranged for a pick up at KegLand in Noble Park. To my delight I found that they will organise a collection locker for you and issue a code number for entry to their pickup area and another code number for your allocated locker, soo easy and convenient.

Now, Fermzilla's packed into the car I couldn't wait to get home.

The first thing I did upon returning home, was convert my two fermenter fridges to accept the Fermzilla's, leaving enough room at the top for a spunding valve with gauge, that was pretty easy.

Then made up two jumper tubes of 6mm ID clear plastic by 1m long with fluid disconnects on one length and, gas disconnects on the other length, for closed transfers.

I fixed to the lid, a Fermzilla pressure kit. This includes two plastic screw on disconnect posts and a floating outlet tube with gauze filter and float plus a spunding valve with pressure gauge and that basically is all that is required.

I set the fridge controller to 23°c and I made up a brew and filled the Fermzilla, prior to attaching the lid I took a sample and placed the hydrometer into it and my reading was around 1050 which was what the brew manufacturer suggested, I was quite amazed at this. Once the temperature showed 22°C, I added the yeast.

I then adjusted the spunding valve so it was just on, let it go and wallah. As the Fermzilla is made from totally clear material it is easy, and interesting, to see what is happening. After just a couple of hours, the brew looked very dark and curd looking, the next day it appeared very, very light looking and very slight krausen (a German word meaning frill) and the spunding gauge showed about 2psi.

On the third day, the brew was a very light caramel colour and I increased the pressure valve slightly, still very little krausen on the top.

On day five the colour was darkening, pressure was showing 12psi and even less krausen, on day seven, the colour was that of black coffee, but appeared clearish so I decided to take a sample of the brew.

I had bought a picnic beer tap and had attached it to a 6mm ID tube about 600mm long, and a fluid disconnect valve, so I could remove a sample without allowing any gas to escape or air to enter.

I connected this tap and the brew entered the float line and then the tap line, placing a glass jug under the tap spout I pulled the lever on the tap.

I could not believe the foamy beer flowing into the jug, at about one third full I, stopped the pouring and I was awe struck at the foamy head on the beer in the jug. The beer was not clear but fairly murky and I poured my sample into the hydrometer tube and placed the hydrometer in, after the foam had settled, I took a reading, which appeared, to me to be around the same as before at 1050.

I left the hydrometer in the sample for about twenty minutes and then took another look. All the froth had now subsided and it now appeared to be around 1025 or more, which was 15 more than the brew manufacturer recommended. I then gingerly tasted the sample and thought it tasted somewhat disgusting.

I then turned the fridge controller down to 3°c, as per the desired temperature to 'cold crash' as I had read on the Fermzilla Facebook page, this would, according to advice, allow the beer to clear and become carbonated after around three days.

It was now day 10, three days since I had turned the fridge to 3°c. The appearance of the brew was now a better, dark coffee looking colour, but not as strong and I could see the floating tube and float quite clearly. I took another sample in the jug and it looked quite good although very hazy with a good head and plenty of bubbles.

I couldn't resist and tasted it, quite good, certainly seemed to have lost its 'home brew' taste that the previous beers sported. I took a SG reading with the hydrometer and seemed to be still around 1025.

As I was removing the hydrometer from the sample, I somehow dropped it, and it landed on the tiled floor with quite an explosion, and a million, or maybe two million tiny balls advanced across the kitchen floor to the lounge room, and then distributed themselves along the hallway to the bedrooms.

I did not replace the hydrometer and from that day on I have never taken another reading by means of a hydrometer (more on this later).

I was of the opinion that the brew was ready to keg even though the hydrometer reading did not agree, anyway it was ten days since I put the brew on and it didn't look too bad so let's do it.

I had three clean kegs and freshly sanitised, I connected the CO_2 gas line from the cylinder to the first kegs inlet post and applied about 3psi to this keg and purged air from it via the pressure relief valve.

I removed the CO_2 line from the kegs inlet post and fitted the spunding valve, with the dial to the kegs inlet post.

Then I released the pressure from the Fermzilla via the relief valve, then fitted the CO_2 line and applied 3psi to the Fermzilla.

I then connected the fluid jumper tube, to the outlet of the Fermzilla, and to the outlet of the keg and, nothing happened, until I slowly, released pressure from the keg using the spunding valve, and we have transfer, albeit slow, it was working, I quickly noted the volume by litre gauge on the Fermzilla and waited while it had shown 19 litres had been transferred.

Excellent so it seemed, and I repeated this fairly simple procedure in turn to the remaining two kegs.

I then placed these three kegs into the kegerator and applied 20 psi to two of the kegs and connected the third kegs inlet post to the CO_2 line and the outlet to the beer tap, set the CO_2 at 7psi, for the beer delivery pressure.

I pulled my first beer from my new, pressure brewed system and I looked disappointingly at the beer I had just pulled. It was cloudy, certainly not clear, as I had expected but definitely not as bad as the previous brews.

I then tasted the beer, quite good, but did not seem to have the 'home brew' or cardboard taste that I found with almost every home brew beer that I have tasted previously.

Very nice taste in fact, but did seem to have a bitter taste that I had also experienced, with my previous natural aspirated brews.

But, this was not too bad in taste. The clarity though was disappointing, and I was hoping this might improve over time in the keg. The clarity did not really improve, but the bitter taste seemed to increase with the next keg and then, strangely, remarkably decrease with the last keg.

It seemed it was still not the beer I wanted due to the bitter taste and, that seemed to change randomly between kegs, and also the clarity. I really believe the clarity, of the beer to be of the essence, for some strange reason, or other, I don't really know why, but to me, a cloudy looking beer is just not my style.

BACK TO THE DRAWING BOARD

I had read about some home brewers, using a filter system that showed excellent results and were most very pleased. But, also read the comments from others also using a filter, claiming that the filtering process not only removed the cloudy appearance but also removed most of the beer's taste.

Others claimed the filter removed the carbonation from the pressure fermenter to some extent.

Whilst similar comments, also included that filters were only necessary for people who drank and tasted, only with their eyes. Seems a very common comment on this one and I think it is a popular smokescreen.

So, how would you know who is right and who is wrong, but, I know what I want and that is clear beer, and I was on a mission.

Back to the KegLand online catalogue and….Wallah…. an affordable beer filtering system that has the following description;

This beer filter is designed to be used with our Absolute 1 Micron Filter. This filter works best when used as the middleman when transferring icy cold (-1°C) un carbonated beer between two kegs. All you will need to do is purchase some hosing, clamps, ball locks and an Absolute 1 Micron Filter to use this system.

If you drink with your eyes and prefer a crystal clear beer, then this really is the cheapest method to getting crystal clear beer with little to no effort.

This system sounds good but does state for the transfer of, uncarbonated, beer and also states that it works best for transferring between kegs.

I thought if this can transfer between kegs then surely it would also transfer between a Fermzilla and a keg, so let's go for it and get a filter.

It just would not work, I hooked it up between my beer delivery line from the Fermzilla to the keg and all it did, was make foam from the filters out line to the keg thus filling the keg with foam.

Failure, what a pity I thought and sought more advice on filtering and found comments from a brewer using this same system explaining, that to transfer carbonated beer through this filter requires the dispensing vessel to have higher pressure than the carbonated beer within and that, the receiving vessel, a slightly less pressure to avoid the beer turning to foam. As an example, a bottle of unopened soft drink has no bubbles, remove the top and it bubbles because the pressure on the surface has been removed.

Well, to me this seems positive; I will try this, seeing as I now own a filter, that to date, is another failure.

Whilst fermenting I have the brew about 12psi for 10 days then at 15psi for 3~4 days whilst cold crashing to 3°c, which brings the pressure down to around 10psi. So, I estimated the brew to be somewhere between 10 and 12psi.

I set up the Fermzilla with the inlet post to the Co2 cylinder line and set to 12psi.

I then turn the tap on the outlet of the filter to, OFF and connect the Fermzilla outlet post line to the filter's inlet.

This will allow the beer to flow into the filter until the beer pressure causes the flow to stop.

I then, apply pressure to the filter's relief valve to expel air leaving the filter full of beer with no froth or air bubbles.

Now connecting the filter's outlet to the kegs outlet (yes, that is correct, filter outlet to keg outlet).

We are ready and, by turning the filter outlet tap to ON, the beer flowed through the clear tube into the keg, excellent, until some bubbles started to appear and then, turned into pure froth from the filter outlet to the keg inlet.

It was then that I noticed a stream of air bubbles emerging from the Fermzilla dip tube, then into the filter causing the filter to fill with Co2........not good I thought.

After watching this stream of bubbles and wondering where it was possibly coming from, I wondered if it may be the carbon dioxide that had been absorbed into the beer that may be of greater pressure than the space above it and causing the bubbles. Yes, just like the soft drink bottle.

I did not really have a clue but thought I would try increasing the Co2 pressure to the Fermzilla to 15psi................the bubbles immediately disappeared, the filter dispelled the gas and filled with beer and the outlet line to the keg became clear, with no froth, ...wallah again!

I completely filled all three kegs this way, then took a one third jug sample from the last keg and it looked to be fairly clear, I then poured this sample into a cold glass from the refrigerator and it looked beautiful, lovely looking head, the beer so clear that I could almost look through the glass and it also had a healthy looking stream of bubbles coming from the bottom of the glass where the nucleation points are etched. I could hardly believe it, I took a sip, great taste really nice taste but! It still had that bitter aftertaste, but otherwise, almost a complete success. This was what I wanted except for the bitter taste.

The bitter taste in the beer was not, I knew, from previous experiments, part of the brewing extract, I now also knew, that it was not an off taste from air contact and I also knew, from previous unsatisfactory kegs that this bitter taste did seem to vary from keg to keg leaving me with the only conclusion,........Dirty Kegs???

I knew the kegs were not dirty, as I had been meticulous in cleaning them (full details on cleaning kegs are detailed later); I had even disassembled the dip tubes and posts to ensure their cleanliness!

I suddenly associated this bitter taste, with the cleaning product I was using on these kegs......Nappisan.

I know that Nappisan, is a great product, as with many similar products incorporating Sodium Per carbonate and other strange chemicals and seems to be quite popular with many brewers, but I thought this may be the source of the bitter aftertaste in my beer and decided to desist with this product but what to use in lieu of?

I consulted a cleaning chemical retailer and outlined my thoughts with respect to the cleaning chemical I was using, and he did not hesitate to say, that residuals from this particular cleaning product, being granulated, does require a great effort in neutralising by lots of clean water rinsing to ensure that all granules have in fact dissolved.

He went on to say that his company, EcoClean Avanti, produced a product (actually made in Queensland) called GW20, which is a formulated beer glass cleaner based on materials, that do not interfere with the head, or the taste of the beer and is also used to clean beer lines.

This looked like another positive way forward and was worth the test. I bought and applied this product to my cleaning methods with the result of the total elimination of the bitter aftertaste in my beer.

It just seemed too simple to be true. The bitter taste was gone. My beer was now perfect, just as I wanted it to be!

After almost eighteen months of trial and error, I now have the situation where I can go to my kegerator and pull a beer into a cold glass from my adjacent refrigerator, and that beer is equally as good, if not better, than a beer served in a commercial environment.

This is what I wanted and I have now achieved it and I can reproduce this in varying tastes and styles with very little effort and very little expense when compared to commercial beer purchase.

What Gear Do You Need

Beer brewing under pressure with the Fermzilla will have your beer ready to drink in about 12 to 14 days.

You can, either drink this directly from the Fermzilla, bottle it with a 'duotight' bottle filler gun or Keg it.

So work out your required quantity and how you propose to store it, bottles or kegs as storage in the Fermzilla puts it out of production until empty.

I choose to store my beer in 19 litre kegs and do not generally bottle any of my brew (I do actually, on occasions, fill PET bottles directly from the beer tap for taking on trips) so it works best for me to brew in 57 litre batches that equals 3 kegs, which requires 2.5 cans of extract at the manufacturers recommended rate of one can for 23 litres (I store the half can in a sealed glass jar in the refrigerator).

So, if your beer consumption is around two cartons of stubbies per week, you need only one 60 litre Fermzilla and three 19 litre kegs, or 76 x 750ml PET bottles, to make one brew of 57 litres each three weeks to ensure an ample supply.

If your consumption is less, then that is also fine as the brew can stay in the Fermzilla at 3°C until required,

I have left beer for over four weeks without any drama, if anything the taste should improve.

Assuming the above consumption rate suits you then the following equipment is all that may be required. I am not including stainless steel mixing bowls, buckets, kitchen scales, stirring utensils and other such items that may already be present in your home.

Kegerator: For up to 3 keg storage. These are available from various companies from, approximately $650.00. This price should include Co2 gauges, beer line, airline and post connectors.

It's your choice for the number of taps you may require. Two minimum I would recommend, as you may want to get an extra keg and produce your own carbonated water, as I do.

Co2 Cylinder: This is required for the closed transfer of beer from the Fermzilla to the kegs and also for the serving pressure to the kegerator beer tap. These vary in size, mostly 2.5 & 6kg, most kegerators seem to accommodate 6kg cylinders. These, including gas, are available at around 2.5kg $70 and 6kg $120 .00.

It is a good idea to have two of these, one for kegerator delivery and one for kegging, which also works as a spare when refilling the other cylinder.

Beer Kegs 19lt: You will need three of these, complete with lids and ball lock posts are available from most outlets at around $110.00 each. Second hand and/or reconditioned, are also available at times for about $60 to $75 each. You will really need three of these to allow for continuous beer production.

Beer Gravity filter system with 1 micron cartridge filter: Some of these are offered for sale complete with 9mm duotight fittings at about $30.00 including cartridge. Make sure you get a washable cartridge, rather than a paper cartridge.

Fermzilla with pressure kit: This is the main fermenter known as the 'all rounder'. The pressure kit includes the posts and the float and outlet tube with a filter. These are available at $95.00. You will also require a 'blowtie' spunding valve kit with a pressure gauge at around $30.00. Note: the float tube will need to be cut to the required length. For my 60 Litre Fermzilla, I have cut the tube to 700mm.

Refrigerator for Fermzilla: Here you can use any type of fridge that is large enough to hold the Fermzilla, but it has to be a dedicated fridge as most of the time it will be running at around 22°C to 24°C, which makes it unsuitable for the storage of any other food or drink.

Refrigerators without a freezer can be found second hand or new as per personal choice so I can't attach a value to this. But a new 240 litre Hisense retails at around $600.

Refrigerator Controller: This will maintain your fridge at the required temperature for fermenting and 'cold crashing, these vary in price from around $50.00.

With the climate where I live, I have no requirement to heat the inside of my fridge to maintain temperatures of around 24°C, in cooler climates you may also require a heating device, 'Heat Belt's' are effective without creating hot spots, these are inexpensive usually below $20.00.

The refrigerator controller has a power inlet for both the fridge and the heater to allow it to maintain the temperature.

There is also a 'Rapt ' controller available, that works in conjunction with the Rapt Pill, mentioned below, by automatically controlling the temperature of your brew from the sensor inside the Fermzilla.

Rapt Pill: I think for the price, about $70.00, this is a must. It floats in your brew in the Fermzilla and connects via Wi-Fi to your iPhone, iPad, laptop or whatever, to give you an ongoing readout on the status of your beer.

Easy to set up and reports on specific gravity, temperature and alcohol content, It also records the brews details that you submit. No more opening your Fermzilla to gain samples and allowing a chance of contamination.

Food Grade Pump: May not be required if you have sufficient room above your Fermzilla in the fridge. I use one for the transfer of my diluted sugars and extract from mixing container to Fermzilla. The one I use is called 'Supa Sucka' and costs around $60.00.

Sanitising Solution & Cleaning Detergents: I use Stella San sterilising solution at about $7 for 500ml that will last you years, and for cleaning all items I use Eco Clean – Avanti GW20 in a 5 litre container for about $50

2 x Tap Kegarator
I use one tap for beer and I keep a keg of carbonated water inside and use the other tap for water

19 Litre Corny Keg

6kg c02 Cylinder
It's a good idea to have two cylinders, one for the kegerator and another for kegging

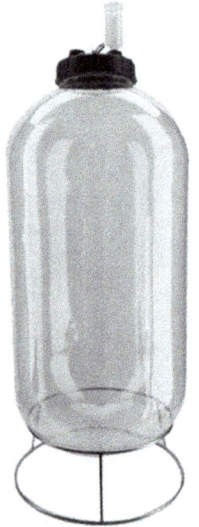

Fermzilla Allrounder 60Lt

Parts required for pressure brewing are a c02 inlet post (red) and an outlet post (yellow) with a floating diptube

Spunding valve for maintaining required pressure in the Fermzilla

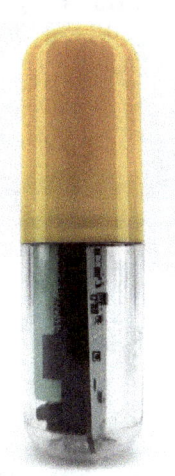

RAPT PILL, reports via Wi Fi on your brews SP, Temperature and ABV plus other reports

FOOD TRANSFER PUMP
A must when using the big 60Lt Fermzilla. This allows the Fermzilla to remain in the refridgerator

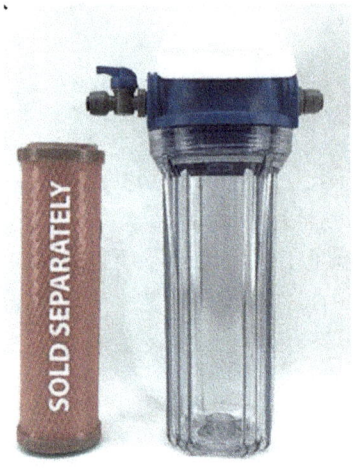

1 Micron Filter
I don't think that filtering is an option and is worth the slight effort

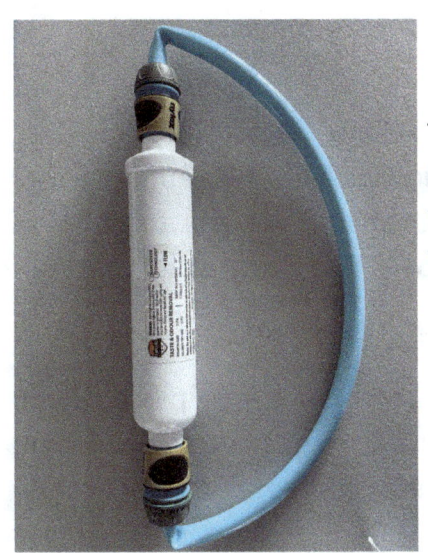

TASTE and ODOUR REMOVAL
Nothing goes into my fermenters without going through this filter

Temperature Controller

A water filter is also a must I think, regardless of what condition your drinking water is in, just as a precaution, filters that click on to tap fittings are available for less than $100, last for about a year and remove all chemical tastes from water.

There will be of course, various other bits and pieces such as a thermometer, extended stirrer for Fermzilla, clear tubing and disconnects for jumper lines and a small manual pump that I use for cleaning.

For the beer transfer from Fermzilla to filter, then filter to keg, I use Duotight disconnects with 9mm push in fittings, on these I have a short length (50mm) of 9mm OD pipe to fit the Duotight fitting with 8mm ID clear tube over the 9mm pipe. I have done this as I was not able to acquire, 9mm OD clear tube, only a coloured tube, (pipe), which does not allow a visual of the flow of bubbles.

These same type of Duotight fittings I have also used on my transfer pump.

All in all, it adds up to approximately $2,500.00, or, you may find second hand kegs and a second hand kegerator as I did for around $1,500.00.

Beware when buying second hand, in the instance of the kegerator, for obvious reasons, for kegs you will want to replace all the O rings and seals, but also check inside for any hard build up from whatever it had previously contained as these may not be removable and could cause for bacterial build up also.

Although, I did buy a second hand fermenter, that was not a pressure fermenter, so be sure, if you happen on a second hand Fermzilla or similar, that it can hold the pressures you will be using, which should be between 10 to 15 psi. Good idea to change the PRV (pressure release valve) down to a 15 psi (purple).

The second hand kegerator that I bought, lasted only about one year and just stopped working. Having no knowledge of its age, I decided that $700 for a new kegerator, complete with new gauges, lines and fittings might be the best way to go. The new kegerator also had a flexible pipe blowing cold air from the fan, up, into the font.

This makes a big difference when pouring beers with respect to froth, as when the beer leaves the keg and flows into a hot beer line it tends to foam.

As with the second hand kegs I have, five in total, I have installed new posts, seals, O-rings and even tubes. When, or if, I have to replace them I think I will go for new kegs.

Beer Glasses: These are also a very important part when it comes to kegging, as you will need to have some way to drink the beer within the keg.

You may have a home with drinking glasses in abundance and beer mugs to burn, but beware, that some of these glasses can really affect your beer to such extreme as to really spoil it.

The main issue here is usually, no head or rapidly disappearing head, followed by flat beer! Ugh……..And,…it could possibly just be that it needs to be cleaned correctly.

Today's, modern beer glasses are etched at the bottom of the glass, which is called a 'Nucleation Point'. This helps the release of carbonation in the beer and generally, creates a steady stream of bubbles emanating from the bottom of the etched portion of the glass. If you do, go buying new beer glasses then make sure you look for this, very hard to see in some instances.

The good news here is, that you can etch your old beer glasses yourself with the aid of a Dremmel, or similar machine that comes with a little diamond tipped bit. If you don't have one, it may be a good excuse to get one rather than buy new glasses.

Regardless, of what type you have, if not cleaned correctly, they won't work!

Just 'Google' it up, 'How to clean beer glasses' and there are quite a few different ideas and systems. But! Think…you don't have problems with glasses at the pubs right, but they use glass washing machines, right, then if you wash at home with the same solution that they use in their machines, then it may work for you too.

I do exactly that, I use, the same, GW20 as I mentioned earlier, combined with a set of three glass, cleaning brushes that are set on a base with suction pads.

This fits perfectly in the kitchen sink, I firstly spray a mixture of 10ml GW20 per one litre of water, made up in a spray bottle, inside and outside of each glass to be washed, then in a revolving motion apply the glass to the brush set, then rinse with fresh water.

CLEANING YOUR GEAR

Generally, all my gear is all kept clean and stored in a clean place until I use it.

Kegs: Once emptied, with the Co2 gas retained inside, are simply placed in a cool place, out of sunlight, until they are required to be filled within a couple of weeks or so. As the kegs are full of gas they should not become contaminated by air.

If they are not going to be filled for some time they should be cleaned upon emptying and then stored in a cool place.

Cleaning kegs: is not as hard as people seem to think, I clean my kegs in the bath (without bath plug) in the bathroom with the shower attachment.

To clean kegs you will need a manual type of air pump with a ball lock post "air", or "in" disconnect fitting attached.

And a short length of 6 or 8mm clear tubing with a ball post "fluid", or "out" disconnect fitting attached.

This clear tube with fluid disconnect I now call the "fluid tube" for the sake of clarity.

Firstly place about 6 litres of water in a plastic bucket and add 10ml of GW20 per litre to the bucket and place the bucket in the bath.

If the keg has previously been in use, then release all CO_2 from the keg and remove the lid, rinse and leave the lid in the bucket of detergent.

Tip any existing residual from the keg into the bath, then using the shower attachment, rinse the inside of the keg, just enough water to rinse around, not more than about 2lt then discard water from the keg.

Using a 1lt plastic jug, or similar, pour 1lt of detergent solution from the bucket into the keg and fit the lid on the keg.

Attach the pump to the keg with the "air" disconnect fitting then apply pressure, about 3~4 psi, into the keg then remove the pump from the post.

Shake the keg vigorously then place the "fluid tube" to the kegs "out" post and allow the detergent mix to freely flow out, this cleans and flushes detergent through the kegs outlet tube.

Disconnect the "fluid tube" and release keg pressure, remove the lid and empty out any remaining detergent from the keg then refit the "fluid tube" and blow with your mouth through the tube to empty the kegs inlet tube of any remaining detergent (it is very important to ensure all detergent is removed from the kegs outlet tube)

Then rinse the lid with water, add a couple of litres of clean water to the keg, shake and empty the keg.

Add another couple of litres of fresh water to the keg and fit the lid, fit the pump as previously and add air pressure. Remove the pump and attach the "fluid tube" and allow rinse water to flow freely. Empty the keg and blow through the "fluid tube" to remove any water

This has now cleaned the keg, its outlet tube and outlet post. We will now sanitise the keg.

Sanitising kegs: Before any cleaning, it's a good idea to mix up some sanitiser.

I use StellerSan, which is a non-rinse sanitiser and I keep it pre mixed in a 15 litre drum with a tap for convenience. I also keep on hand, a full 1 litre spray bottle filled with the mixed sanitiser.

To sanitise all three kegs, and later the Fermzilla, I use only one litre of sanitiser

(Many brewers totally fill the keg with sanitiser; I find no reason for this).

Place sanitiser into a 1 litre jug and pour into the cleaned keg, fit the keg lid, attach the pump and apply pressure.

Remove the pump and attach the "fluid tube", with the open end of the fluid tube in the jug you have poured the sanitiser from, this is so the sanitiser can be reused.

(You don't have to reuse the sanitiser; you can use fresh sanitiser if you wish).

Once all of the sanitiser has been transferred from the keg and only air emits from the keg you are ready to fill the keg. Do not remove the lid.

General Cleaning Agent

10ml per litre

For cleaning Kegs and Fermenter

I use 50ml of GW20 to 5LT of water mixed in a bucket.

This is enough to clean; 3 x 19Lt Kegs and the 60Lt Allrounder

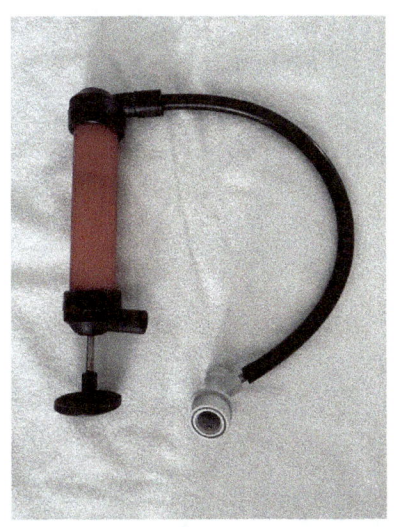

Air Pump

With IN disconnect

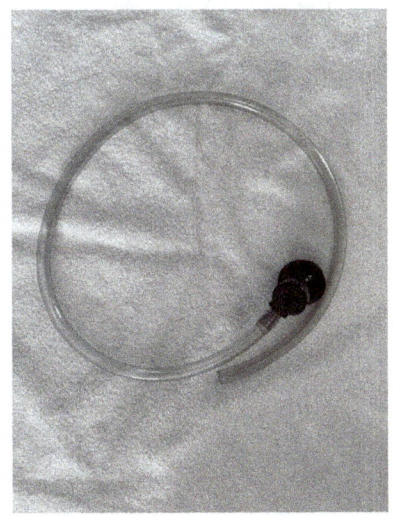

Fluid Tube

After rinsing keg

Add 1 Litre of GW20 Mix

Then fit lid of keg

Fit Pump and add approx 5~8 psi (just guess it)

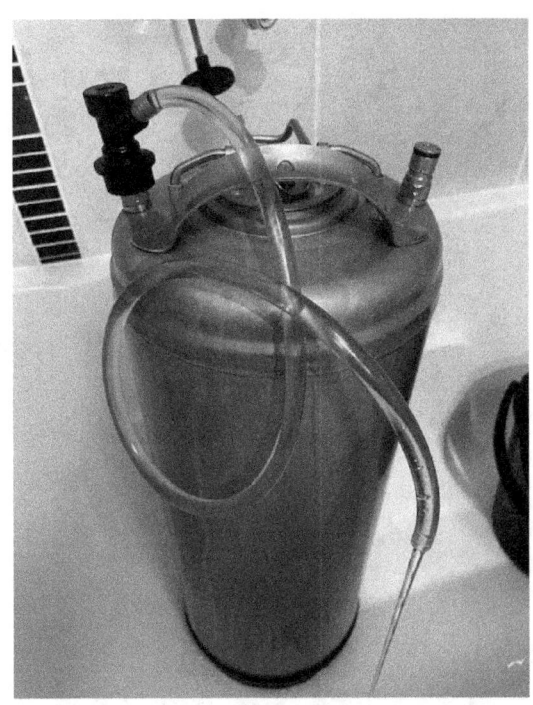

Detergent is flowing through 'Fluid Tube"

When empty, remove lid and hold tube upright, or blow through tube, **Important to ensure all detergent is removed from the Keg's tube.**

<u>*Repeat this stage with fresh water following a rinse-out of detergent,*</u> **Important make sure you remove the water from the keg tube**

Final **Stage**

Pour 1 litre of Stella San mixture into clean Keg

Fit Keg Lid

Shake vigorously

Fit pump and add pressure

Remove pump and fix 'Fluid Tube' to OUT post

Allow sanitiser to flow back into jug for reuse

Do Not Remove Keg Lid

Beer Filter: This is the only time I use the Per Carbonate based detergent (Nappisan or similar).

You will need to make up a connection to fit from your water tap to the out tube on your filter to simply 'backwash ' the filter until the water runs clear.

Following backwashing, remove the filter lid and cartridge, remove washers or gaskets from the top and bottom of the cartridge and O ring seal from the filter housing and rinse as required to remove any dirt or buildup.

Place one desert spoon of Nappisan (or similar) into the base of the filter housing then add about 200ml of clean water, mix this solution with a wooden, or plastic stirrer, until dissolved, refit washers, gaskets to the cartridge and refit O ring seal to filter housing, place cartridge into the filter housing, fill with water and then fit filter lid.

Leave this soaking for overnight, or longer, then remove the filter cartridge, remove the washers, gaskets then rinse the cartridge thoroughly. I find the best way to do this, and 'don't laugh' is place the cartridge into your toilet cistern and leave for two days, then turn the cartridge around (upside down) and leave for a further 2 days, due to regular water movement this process should remove any trace of the Per Carbonate detergent. Remove and allow to dry.

(Of course, check your toilet cistern condition first as it may need a clean out before using this to flush your filter).

Before use, spray sanitiser around the inside of the filter housing, the filter lid, including the inlet and outlet ports and the cartridge including washers, gaskets and O ring seal.Fermzilla: I don't clean my Fermzilla, until immediately after emptying into kegs.

Do not leave Fermzilla for any length of time without releasing pressure down to 3 psi, after emptying into keg/kegs, as the pressure will build rapidly once the Fermzilla starts to warm up following cols crashing to 3°c.

When empty, release Co2 pressure to about 3psi then use the lid opening tool (available from KegLand) to release the locking ring slowly until Co2 escapes around the lid seal, this should raise the lid from the Fermzilla for easy removal (DO NOT ATTEMPT THIS WITHOUT FIRST RELEASING PRESSURE TO 3psi OR LESS).

Completely remove the locking ring and remove the lid, remove the outlet tube with float and filter intact, rinse with clean water and place in a bucket with detergent.

Carefully remove Rapt Pill, if using from Fermzilla, rinse with clean water and place in a bucket with detergent.

Rinse the residual in the base of Fermzilla, shake and discard, you don't need much water to do this as, the more water you use, the harder it is to handle, continue to rinse and discard until the water is clear.

Pour about 1litre of detergent mixture from the bucket into the Fermzilla and slosh around, at this stage, if there are any persistent marks anywhere inside, wipe with a soft wet cloth, do not use anything even slightly abrasive as this may leave minute scratches that can house bacteria.

Tip out the detergent and rinse Fermzilla a few more times, turn upside down to drain for a few minutes, then using the 1litre of sanitiser left over from keg cleaning, or use fresh sanitiser, pour into Fermzilla and slosh around ensuring sanitiser comes into contact with all internal Fermzilla walls.

Pour sanitiser from Fermzilla back into the jug (there is one more job left for this sanitiser unless it has become dirty) and place Fermzilla upside down to completely drain.

Don't worry about the soapy appearance around the inside of the Fermzilla if you are using StellarSan as this tasteless.

Place Fermzilla back on its base in the refrigerator and fill to desired quantity with filtered cold water. Spray sanitiser around the rim of the Fermzilla then using a piece of cling wrap approximately 200x200mm also spayed with sanitiser, place over the rim of Fermzilla, sanitiser side down, and lightly place locking ring over this to avoid any foreign articles entering Fermzilla.

Adjust the refrigerator controller to the required setting and ready for the next brew.

That is generally all that is required for cleaning other than flushing out your tubes and then sanitising for kegging.

To flush tubes immediately after use, connect a "carbonation and line cleaning" ball lock fitting (the same fitting that comes with the Fermzilla carbonation kit, an extra one will cost around $4), and flush with fresh water, then flush with sanitiser. Replace these tubes if they become brown or dirty inside, mine haven't yet after two years of use.

As I said, I do not clean anything until I am ready to use it other than the filter and filter cartridge and any beer tubes, unless items are not going to be used for more than a week or two. If you are not putting on another brew within a week, or so, after kegging, then you should clean the Fermzilla and thoroughly dry it after use, then rewash and sanitise prior to use.

If kegs are left complete with the CO_2 within them after dispensing, then they should not become contaminated, unless they leak.

I don't start kegging until I am satisfied the fermentation is complete, then, the cold crashing is successful and then kegging starts with cleaning and follows through to Fermzilla cleaning, filling with water then re brewing, all in the scope of around 3.5 hours from start to finish.

I, like most I would think, do not like cleaning the kegs, or the Fermzilla, which all up takes about… 3 kegs at 10 mins each = 30 minutes, Fermenter, all of 10 mins, in total 35mins, depending on how many breaks in between, then filling the fermenter = 10 mins

I don't mind kegging; I sit and have a beer, or two, and take about an hour, to one and a half, to fill.

Making the brew, around an hour, adding the brew to the Fermzilla, then the yeast, stirring, fitting the lid and whatever else about 30 mins, all up about 3.5 hours.

The only other cleaning required will be your beer glasses.

Where to brew

If you don't prepare your food in the garage, garden shed, or under your carport, then why brew your beer in those environments?

Believe me, you don't need a lot of room for brewing, fermenting and kegging your beer. And that is what we are making BEER, it's a food don't forget and as such requires a clean, healthy environment. Such as your kitchen for brewing, maybe your laundry to keep your fridge that will house your Fermzilla, it will most likely be big enough to do your kegging as well. But! Somewhere clean.

My wife and I now live in a two bedroom apartment, it's all we require and the second bedroom and bathroom make it ideal when we have guests.

So, where do I make beer?

Mixing the extract and the sugars, in the kitchen, you only need room for two mixing bowls that can handle up to 8 litres each.

My Fermzilla fridges, yes fridges, as I run two Fermzilla's, are located in the second bedroom, inside the wardrobe with the glass sliding doors, there is one fridge on each side of the robe with shelving in between. I can't access both fridges at the same time, as the sliding doors won't allow it, but it works well for me.

To fill the Fermzilla, I have a double, screw on, attachment, they are available at Bunnings, on the washing machine water outlet tap that I connect a food grade, 10mm hose with snap on connectors and a tap on the delivery end.

To add the mixed extract and sugars to the Fermzilla, I have the food grade pump, mentioned in the equipment chapter, and I sit these on a fold up table in front of the fridge and pump in to the Fermzilla. I use a clamp to hold the pump to the table.

I clean up all kegs and Fermzilla in the second bathroom with the flexible shower hose and head.

To fill the kegs, when kegging, in the second bedroom room, I simply stand all three kegs in a flat, tray type container, they are available from most two dollar type shops, to retain any condensation dripping down the kegs when filling.

LET'S DO IT

Assuming that you have put together all the required equipment, as shown in the required gear section, you now need the ingredients for the brew.

The following are the ingredients for **two** 57 litre brews.

Extract: x 5 cans of 1.7kg. Here you can use any type you may fancy with respect to Lager, Ale's and Pilsener's and any brand you wish. The only types that I have used to date are Coopers Lager, Morgans Lager, Morgans Premium Lager, Morgans Pilsener and Morgans Qld Gold. I have enjoyed all of these but tend to settle on Morgans Qld Gold, this brew strongly resembles, we think, Great Northern Super Crisp that you will get on tap in the venues. Each ex Cairns 20.00, ex Vic 18.50.

Dextrose: x 3kg, I buy this in 4.5kg packs, it works out the value and it provides for 3 x brews. Kg price ex Cairns 3.20, ex Vic 2.90.

Corn Syrup: (Maltodextrin) x 1.5kg, I get this as 2 x 500 gr. and 2 x 250 gr. easier than weighing out as I find this stuff very messy to weigh. Kg ex Cairns 9.31, ex Vic 3.50

Yeast: Safale US-0 5 x 11.5 gr this yeast is, as the name would indicate, is dedicated to brewing Ale type beers, however, I find it great in Lager and Pilsener beers. I do not use the yeast that comes with the brew; if you try it you may not get the same results that I would expect you to get by following my recipe. Who knows, you may get better. Pack price ex Cairns 6.95. Ex Vic 4.50 (*When I can't get Safale, I use Morgans American Ale Yeast*), I know that some will say that I should be using a lager yeast and that may be fine, but I have used lager yeasts and I much prefer the Ale yeasts that I have nominated.

Other than water, this is all that is required, 4 ingredients, now it's starting to even sound simple.

Looking at the ingredient costs, in Cairns $156 for 114 litres = $1.36 litre, we will add $0.15 per litre for incidentals such as Co2, detergents and sanitiser which brings it to $1.51 litre or, $0.64 per schooner (425ml). That equates to $32.55 per carton of 24 stubbies of 375ml

Cost in Vic, (less freight costs) $129 for 114 litre = $1.13 litre plus incidentals at $0.15 litre = $1.28 litre, $0.54 per schooner (425ml) that equates to $11.52 per carton of 24 stubbies of 375ml.

If your brew turns out like mine and you like it, then that is a very good price to pay for beer.

Presently, September 2023, here in Cairns, to buy a schooner at the club is $8, which is $7.36 more than I pay for it by home brewing.

The current cost of a carton of Great Northern Super Crisp stubbies from Dan Murphy's is $49.95. My home brew equivalent in bottles, I would be saving $38.43.

And……my beer is as good, or better!

Before we can begin to mix any ingredients for the brew, you need to have water in the Fermzilla. Regardless of the condition of your drinking water, all water used for brewing should, in my opinion, be filtered.

Now, don't let this next part about water temperature confuse you, it's not that bad, but very important.

We are going to make a brew of 57 litres; we need to work out how much water to add to the Fermzilla. We will later also need to add our mixed sugars and extract to this water, which will have been mixed with hot water.

Bearing in mind, that we cannot add yeast to this brew until the total mix is between 12° and 24°C. Ideally, 22°C is the temperature to add the particular yeast we are using. Getting your brew to the correct temperature prior to adding yeast is most probably the trickiest part of this whole exercise. It just needs a little calculating to get it right.

Here, where I am brewing, the water temperature from the tap is currently 26°C, so, It is already above the requirement of 22°C. and I have yet to add the mixed sugars and the mixed extract which temperature will be around 50°C, which, of course, will raise my water temperature to about 30°C, so I have to cool my water down to around 17°C to allow the total mixed temperature to be close to 22°C. A little tricky, but just follow this calculation below, you don't have to be over accurate.

The total end result will be 57 litres of beer, so here we will make a total volume of 58 litres of brew mix to allow for the 'crud', the leftover residuals at the bottom of the Fermzilla.

The total fluid in the mixed sugars and extract, for this brew will be.

Extract cans of 1.7kg = 1.25 litres x 2.5 cans = 3.125 litres water 2 litres of hot and 1 litre of cold (or hot depending on water temp) Mixed sugars of 2.25kg with 2 litres hot water added, come to 3.125lt. Total volume to add to water will be (rounded out is near enough) 9 litres, so let's keep it easy and call it 10 Litres.

The amount of water we should put into the Fermzilla will be 45 litres, That will allow 3 litres to add, either hot or cold, for minor discrepancies and temperature adjustments. We fill the Fermzilla to only 45 Litres Of Water, then adjust the water temperature, with the controller, to between 16° and 18° degrees Celsius. **Don't start mixing any ingredients until you have this ready**. Place, cling wrap over the top of the Fermzilla whilst the water temperature is adjusting, to keep anything from getting into the water.

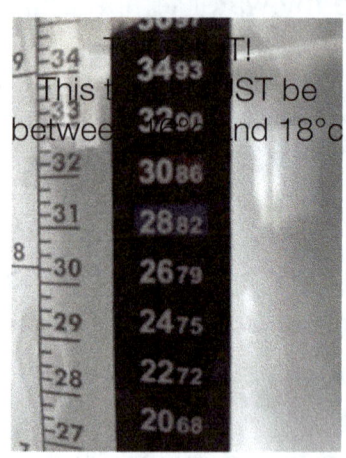

This t... ST be
betwee... nd 18°c

To calculate the total water temperature of two mixtures, multiply the mass and temperature of the first container together and add it to the product of the mass and temperature of the second container. Finally, take that result and divide it by the sum of the masses of water of each container.

So, before I brew I must get the water temperature in the Fermzilla correct. I simply turn the fridge controller to the calculated temp and wait until it reaches the desired temp.

BEFORE, I START MIXING THE SUGARS AND EXTRACT FOR THE BREW. THE WATER TEMPERATURE MUST BE CORRECT.

You can't leave your mixtures to cool else they will create their own cultures whilst mixing with air and this will totally RUIN your BEER. *This can happen very quickly.*

You can cool them, by adding cold water. You can play around with your calculations until you are happy to either cool down or heat up your mixtures, or both the water and the mix. Depending on your climate you may even need to heat the water before adding your hot mixtures.

Just stick with my calcs at 45 litres water at 16~18°c and mixtures at 40~50°c and you won't be too far out.

Ready to start:

Fermzilla filled to 45 litres with filtered water at 18°c.

Transfer pump, including suction pipe and transfer tube sanitised ready to go.

Prepare the following, making sure they are clean and sprayed with sanitiser.

2 x stainless steel containers with a volume of at least 10 litres.

1 x flat stirrer, can opener and a food thermometer,

We are going to use 2.5 cans of extract.

Place 3 unopened cans of extract into the kitchen sink, or whatever with the paper wrapper removed and cover with hot water to soften up the liquid.

Place 750 gr of Maltodextrin (corn syrup) into a mixing container, of at least 10 litre capacity, then add 2 litres of very hot, filtered, water (don't add the Maltodextrin to the water, or you will be mixing for a long, long time) and stir until dissolved. Should go translucent.

Next, the Dextrose, Add 1500 gr (1.5kg), of Dextrose slowly to the Maltodextrin, then stir until totally clear. Set this mixture aside.

Using a glass jar of 750ml capacity with a lid or seal, pour 625ml (half of the can) of extract from the can into the jar and seal immediately. This will be the half can for the next brew. Keep this refrigerated.

Place 2 litres of very hot, filtered, water, into a container, of at least 10 litre capacity, then slowly add 2.5 cans of extract whilst stirring, with a clean stirrer.

Check temperatures of both mixtures and adjust, if required, to between 45~50°C.

Using the transfer pump, immediately transfer the extract mix to the sanitised Fermzilla followed by the sugars mix. The sooner you do this the better as both these mixes can become quickly contaminated.

Using the, sanitised, extended stirrer, stir the brew in the Fermzilla ensuring a uniform colour throughout, this may take up to three minutes.

Once the brew is of a consistent colour, add to the top of the brew, 2.5 packs of the Sofale US-05 yeast. You can guess the half pack or, better still, if you have a really good weighing scale, measure 5.75 gr of yeast from one pack into a sealed container, then pour the balance from that pack into the brew.

Stir this yeast in using a flat stirrer or, similar. The extended stirrer is unsuitable for this part. Stir until completely, dissolved, this may take a few minutes.

Two Extract Cans, with labels removed, in hot water to allow extract to flow easily.

The glass jar contains a half can of extract from previous brew.

Clean Stainless Steel containers sprayed with Stella San

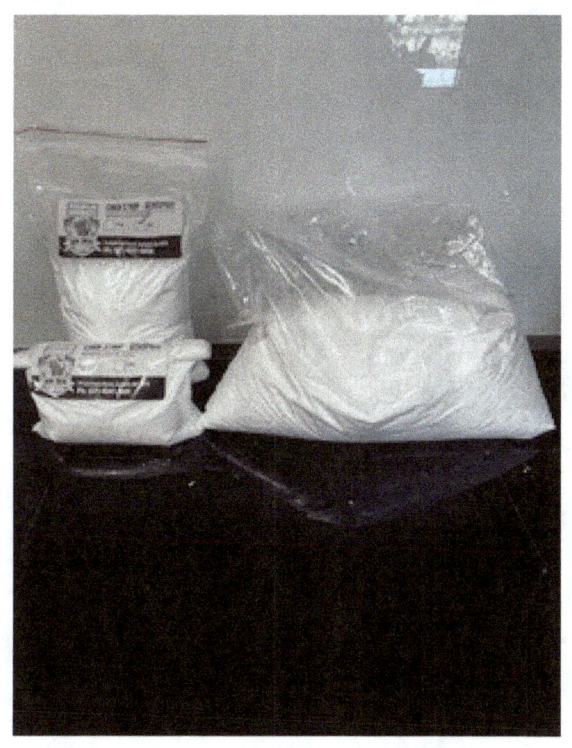

750 gram of Maltodextrin (Corn syrup) to the left

1.5 Kilogram of Dextrose

It's best to have these contents pre weighed and ready

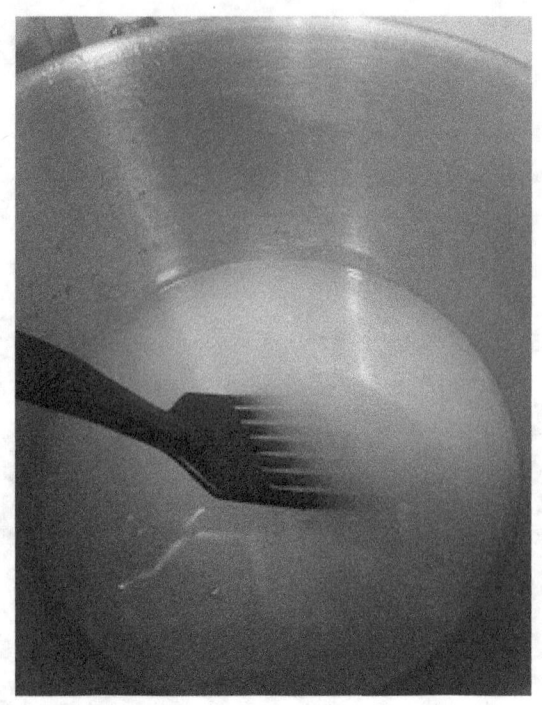

Hot water poured over Maltodextrin and stirred to dissolve

You will not want to add the Maltodextrin to the water as this makes it very difficult to dissolve

Maltodextrin dissolved in hot water should be translucent

Dextrose added to Maltodextrin and starting to dissolve, this will be added to the Fermzilla following the Extract

2.5 cans of Extract added to hot water in the second container, the temperature of this will be adjusted by adding cold water

Extract is being pumped from container into Fermzilla

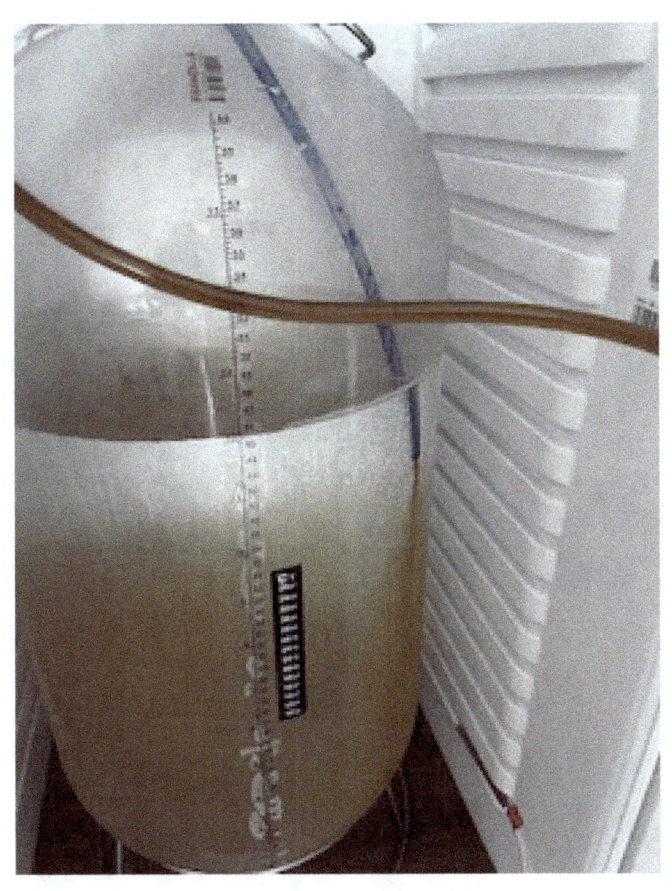
Extract entering Fermzilla

Mixture being pumped from container sugars

Sugars mixture entering Fermzilla

Additional COLD water required for Fermzilla level is added through the pump which will also clean the pump and it's lines

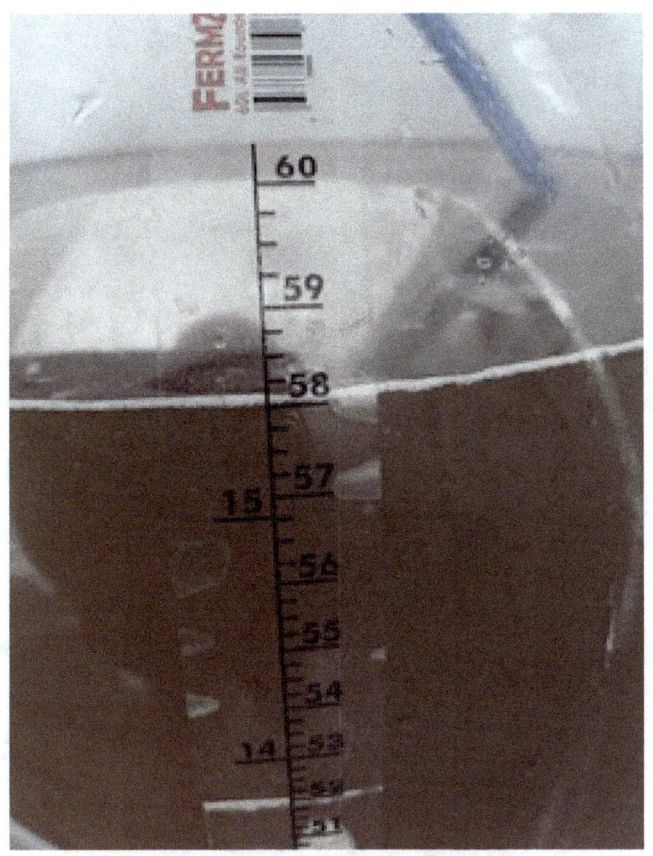

Cold water added to bring the Fermzilla level to 58 litres, 57 litres are required for three 19 litre kegs, 1 litre is to compensate for the bottom residual

Completion of extract and sugar mixture pumping to Fermzilla

Extract and sugars mixed uniformly with hand paddle, whirlpool created to add yeast

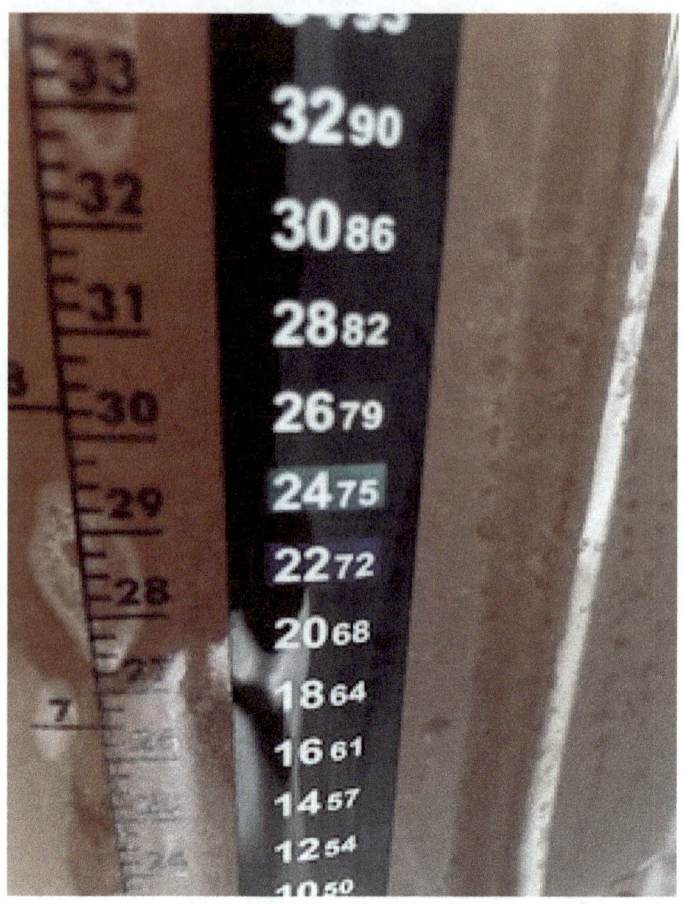

Temperature check prior to adding yeast shows our calculation to be pretty close and we are within the temperature range for the yeast

Yeast added to vortex

Vortex distributes the yeast, ready for thorough mixing with small stirring tool to create air bubbles to stimulate yeast activity

Yeast is completely mixed and is barely visible

Cleaned and sanitised Rapt pill (red item visible) is added to Fermzilla

Cleaned and sanitised float and dip tube is attached to the underside of the yellow OUT post

The lid seal has been lubricated with vaseline then sprayed with sanitiser

This part of the locking ring (pointed out by the scissors) has been lubricated with vaseline the sprayed with sanitiser. This assist's greatly in sealing the lid with light hand pressure only.

It also assist's in the removal of the lid with slight Co2 pressure remaining in the Fermzilla to allow the lid to remove itself from the neck of the Fermzilla and release remaining pressure whilst the locking ring is still threaded

Locking ring attached and tensioned by light hand pressure

When turning the locking ring on the lid, resistance will be found at 2 stages, the first resistance will be felt as the lid engages into the Fermzilla neck, then when continuing to turn the resistance will cease and then start again when the rubber seal engages into the neck, it will then only require minimal hand pressure until the locking ring fully seats

The
Rapt Pill should be sprayed with sanitiser before carefully placing it into the Fermzilla.

The Fermzilla lid should be sprayed with sanitiser and sanitiser should be poured through the inside of the lid's posts by means of the "fluid tube" (mentioned under the cleaning chapter). Sanitiser should then be passed inside the float tube, and then outside the whole float tube, float and filter sprayed with sanitiser.

Before attaching the float tube to the underside of the Fermzilla's 'out' post, smear a little Vaseline, similar around the lid seal (located at the edge of the lid) and also to the underside of the locking ring flange (where it engages the lid), this will allow for easier removal later.

Next, attach the float tube to the lid, one light spray of sanitiser around the seal (over the lubricant) and around the lid, then carefully place the float into the brew and settle the lid on top of the Fermzilla. Place the locking ring on the lid and slowly tighten.

As you tighten you will feel two parts of resistance, once as the lid seats into the rim of the Fermzilla, then after a couple of more turns, the seal enters the rim. A couple more turns till it's firm and that is tight enough, there is no need to over tighten as once the seal is in position, there can be no leakage.

Now time to reset the temperature controller to 22°c.

You must now fit a clear tube with an 'air disconnect' fitted to one end and the other, open end, placed into a glass jar filled with the sanitiser, left over from cleaning to the 'in' post on the lid.

This is to boost the fermentation start and to let you know it has started, which will be seen and heard, within 12 to 24 hours by the vigorous bubbling in the glass jar of the Co2 escaping from the brew. Once this is observed then the

spunding valve should be fitted in lieu of the tube and jar. Set the spunding valve to around 10~12 psi.

Your brew is on and there is now very little for you to do until around 7 days, to increase the Co2 pressure to around 15 psi, then relax until about 14 days till keg time to 'cold crash' then keg. At about day 10 ~ 12, your beer is ready for kegging, your Rapt Pill will show your Specific Gravity has been dormant for a few days, It doesn't really matter if this reading is not what the manufacturer states.

Even if you are not using a Rapt Pill, after 10 days your brew will look dark and fairly clear looking like the pic below and it just looks 'ready'.

It is not crucial that your brew has not completed fermentation when you are kegging as it will just keep on fermenting in the keg, which is unlikely after cold crashing without the danger of exploding, unlike bottling.

Specific gravity seems to drop rapidly when you cold crash. The Rapt Pill chart shows an SG of 1021 after 8 days and a temperature of 21.5°c, when this temperature drops to 3°c the SG will most likely drop to below 2010.

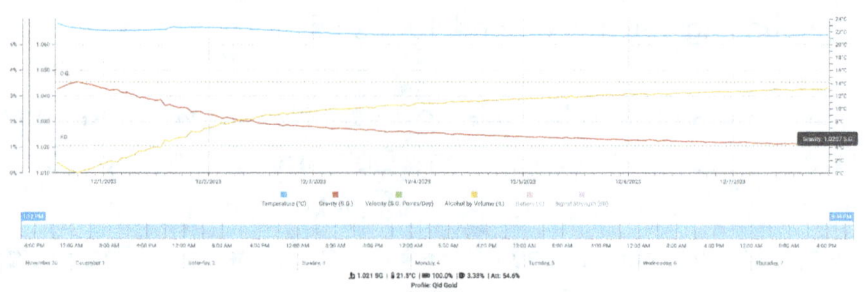

The Rapt Pill chart above can be easily read and the information I am most interested in(from Experience) is The Temperature, The Specific Gravity and the Alcohol By Volume. I do not understand the Attenuation reading and it seems to be most inconsistent from any where between 70 and 85% when I have cold crashed without any difference in taste to the beer

If you don't have a Rapt Pill, you can attache a 'picnic tap' to the yellow OUT post and draw a sample for an SG test.

A drinking test is not a good idea as the temperature will be above 20°

When it looks like this after 8 to 10 days you will just know it is ready to cold crash down to 3°…………well should be!

This beer can now be 'cold crashed', that means, brought down to 3°C, simply set your temperature controller to 3°C, then wait until your Rapt Pill shows the temperature to be 3°C.

This Rapt Pill reading tells me this beer is almost ready to keg, it's actually, almost ready to drink!

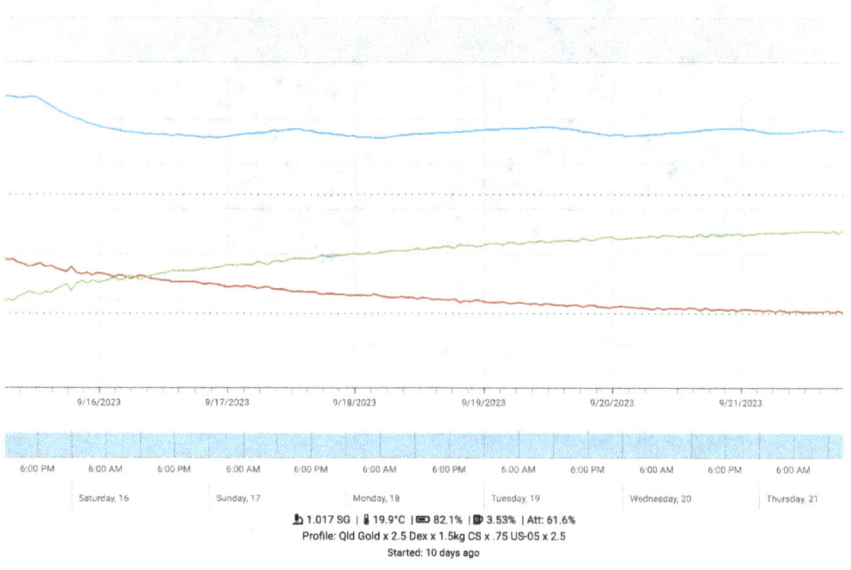

Caption

The bottom two lines of printed data are;

1,017 is the specific gravity, if you look at the red line on the graph, it shows the SG started just above 1,040 at start of brewing, went down to 1,017 and remained there for about 3 days, so it's safe to assume it won't go any lower until It is cold crashed, then it may go lower.

Temperature is reading 19.9°C, dropping now for cold crashing. Battery life is at 82.1%, this is after about 9 brews, so it won't need charging for a while yet.

ABV, alcohol by volume, is at 3.53%, so it is a mid strength beer, might increase slightly on the high side, but just fine.

The last reading shows the Attenuation, I have looked this up and, it seems to mean the yeast's performance.

Then the profile, this is my input so I know what brew I am doing.

The Rapt Pill also creates a log, or history, of previous brews that is easy to access. It is also fairly easy to install and KegLand, are very helpful and available for advice.

There is also a Facebook page 'Rapt Pill Users' another great source for info.

As mentioned earlier, there is also available from KegLand, a 'Rapt' temperature controller that works in conjunction with the Pill. This came out after I had already purchased my controller and I am nowhere near ready to update, but if you are about to start buying gear, get onto the Rapt Pill Users on Facebook.

When you have finished filling your kegs, the Fermzilla pressure will most likely be around the 12~15 psi range and your refrigerator door will be open and depending on your ambient temperature the Fermzilla pressure may increase well past its PRV value of 35 psi and hopefully your Fermzilla is in excellent condition and the PRV will do its job. The same applies if you are using a filter, its pressure will also increase marginally and may blow off your fittings.

Just be cautious and release all pressures once kegging has concluded. Its could also be a clever idea to change the PRV's to 15 psi

KEGGING

You have been dreaming about this, and it's nothing to be worried about, quite easy, lets do it!

In my situation, I will have 3 recently finished and enjoyed empty 19 litre kegs that now require cleaning, so as in the cleaning section of this book, we get them ready for kegging.

Believe me, this is the only way to go, clean and sanitise just before you keg.

Three kegs are in line, in the box. (This is a 750 long x 350 wide x 140mm high poly storage container, less the lid)

Remove the spunding valve and gauge from the Fermzilla's 'in' post.

In the first keg, I will put 12 psi of Co2, from my kegging C02 cylinder, then release the pressure valve on the kegs lid. Then replace the 12 psi of Co2 and fit the "Co2 jumper tube" as described in the Gear chapter.

The gauge side of the jumper with the 'Air' post fitting, to the kegs 'in' post, then the end of the jumper tube with the "fluid" fitting to the next (second) kegs 'out post. Then, on the second kegs "in" post, fit the spunding valve and gauge from the post of the Fermzilla's lid.

Fit the Co2 Cylinder line to the Fermzilla's 'in' post; turn on the Co2 cylinder to 12 psi.

Your filter, which was cleaned immediately after use, as described in section cleaning, now needs to be disassembled and sprayed inside the housing, the cartridge and the top, including the inlet and outlet, with sanitiser. The cartridge and gaskets and O-ring inserted and the top installed, using the tool supplied with the filter. This needs to be fairly tight but not over tight, good idea to keep this tool handy in case you need to adjust the top in case of a leak. Once assembled it is best to place this in a bucket.

The transfer tubes now need to be sanitised, this is best with a post cleaner connection fitted the transfer tubes disconnect fitting and spaying sanitiser down the open end until it appears at the post cleaner fitting.

Fit the transfer tubes to the filter, leaving the post cleaner fitting on the filter outlet (this is to allow purging of the filter).

Everything should now be ready to begin transfer to the first keg.

Connect the transfer tube from the filter's inlet to the Fermzilla's outlet and beer should begin to flow immediately into the filter, as the beer flow slows, gently push the red button on the top of the filter to bleed the filter of air.

Carefully start to open the tap on the outlet side of the filter, just enough to start a flow and allow any residing water to flow through the post cleaner attached to the outlet transfer tube, once clear beer starts to flow, turn off the tap and remove post cleaner, attaché disconnect fitting to 'out' post on the first keg.

Immediately check the Fermzilla's fluid level gauge, it should have gone from 58 litres to 57 litres to fill the filter. Doesn't have to be spot on!

Turn on the filter's outlet tap and beer should now be flowing through the transfer tube to the keg, some visible bubbles, and maybe a little froth, are normal at the start and should clear quickly.

Check the transfer tube on the inlet side of the filter, from the Fermzilla, there should be no bubbles or froth.

If bubbles appear in this tube, increase $Co2$ to 14 psi, and the bubbles should cease.

Check the spunding valve gauge on the $Co2$ jumper tube and adjust it to 12psi, as with the spunding valve gauge on the second keg. Escaping air from the spunding valve on the second keg is normal at about 12 psi.

If you are getting froth from the filter on the outlet side to the keg you may have to increase the pressure on the kegs spunding valve slightly.

Monitor the kegs beer volume by the Fermzilla's fluid gauge, the first keg should show as 38 litres when full, another indicator is the condensation forming on the kegs side, the fluid is generally a little above this mark so be careful and go by calculations from the gauge on the Fermzilla to avoid an overfill. And mess!

Start the second keg fill. It should be about 38 litres showing on the Fermzilla's gauge. Disconnect the transfer tube from the keg and fit it to the second kegs 'Out" post, then change the spunding valve jumper and the spunding valve gauges over to the second and third kegs, the same as when we started.

If transfer is good, then no bubbles or froth will be visible in the transfer tubes, the only indication of flow may be the Fermzilla volume gauge dropping, slowly is better. Allow about 10~15 minutes per keg, no rush.

Transfer to the third keg when the Fermzilla gauge shows 19 litres.

This will still allow for about 1 litre remaining, as residual in the Fermzilla and there should be around a litre of beer left in the filter, to place 19 litres in the keg.

When the float settles on the top of the residual, the gauze will also lay flat and allow only the fluid above it to be transferred through the dip tube, once the fluid is exhausted then only $Co2$ will move through the tube. Allow this to happen until the filter empties, then remove the transfer tube from the keg.

When the brew is looking like this with the pressure at 15psi and everything is telling me that it is ready to cold crash, generally at between 8 to 10 days, then it is time to turn our fridge down to 3°c

We turn down the temperature by adjusting the Temperature Controller from 22°c to 3°c. I generally allow about 2 or 3 days for it to cool

Disconnect the Co2 and the transfer tube from the Fermzilla and release pressure from the Fermzilla down to about 3 psi, this is because the Fermzilla will start to warm up from 3°C to the ambient room temperature and will rapidly increase in pressure. Also, release all pressure in the filter by pushing the red button until there is no pressure, this will avoid the increasing pressure from blowing the transfer tube fittings off. Very messy!

Before, placing kegs into kegerator or fridge, or if you have already done so, release all pressure in each keg by the means of the pressure release valve, PRV on the keg lid, (this is the highest point of outlet for any air that may remain in the keg) careful here in case you may have overfilled slightly as you could get beer spraying out.

Then connect the Co2 Cylinder to the 'in' post on the keg and apply 25 psi, (this extra pressure should ensure a seal to the keg), leave the line connected to the post then turn off the cylinder tap and watch the Co2 gauges for a about 15 seconds to ensure there are no leaks. Leaks, if any are generally fixed by increasing the Co2 pressure to around 35psi.

No loss of pressure on these gauges indicates that the keg is not leaking. That wasn't so scary now, was it ?.....Kegs in kegerator, or fridge to keep cool, now.........one last job.

Clean the transfer lines and the filter, remove the Fermzilla lid (carefully) and remove the dip tube and float, then remove the Rapt Pill (and cancel out on your computer), clean and refill the Fermzilla with water to put another brew on tomorrow, that's right, tomorrow, or as soon as your water temperature is at 18°C. IT BEGINS AGAIN!

This is actually my other Fermzilla, but what I want to demonstrate is the different appearance that the brew takes on once it reaches 3°c.

First thing you will notice is that is has become much clearer

The second thing you will notice is that the pressure has dropped from 15 psi to about 8 psi, this is normal as the Co2 contracts as it becomes cold, you can top this pressure back up to 15 psi if you are not kegging immediately.

Your beer at this stage is very drinkable and a sample should show it, there is no urgent rush to keg this beer and it can be left in this state for quite some time and Co2 can be added for serving pressure

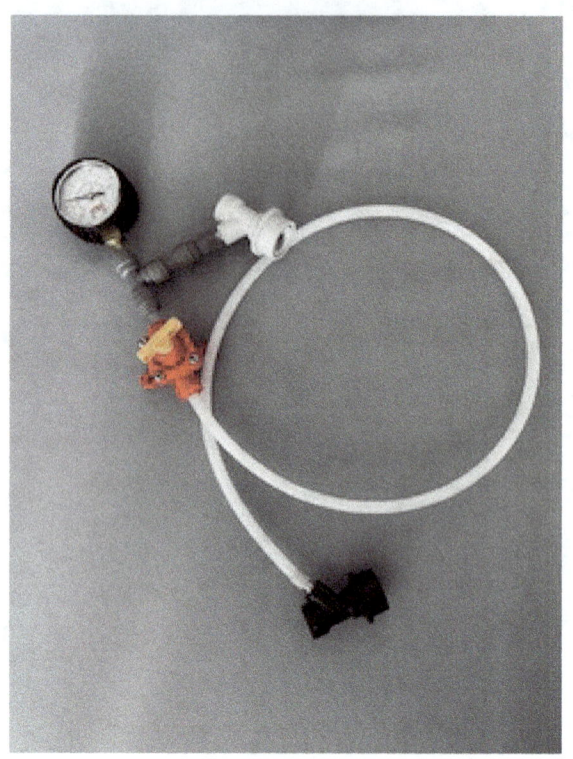

Co2 'Jumper' as can be seen consists of an IN disconnect, a gauge, spunding valve and an OUT disconnect

It's purpose is to charge the following keg with Co2 from the keg being filled, it's benefit being to cut down on the use of Co2 and eliminates the need to manually purge kegs of air

The first keg (lowermost in the pic) has been charged with about 12 psi of Co2. The Co2 'Jumper' has been fixed to this kegs IN post and to the next kegs OUT post, a Spunding valve is also attached to the next kegs IN post

There is no need to purge these kegs of air as the Co2 being the heavier gas will go directly to the bottom of the keg and discharge the air in the keg as it is filled with beer

After sanitising, the filter is assembled and the transfer tube attached

The bucket prevents any condensation spills

The red button is on the filters inlet for purging air from the filter

The filter inlet tube is now connected to the Fermzilla's outlet post, the filter has been filled with beer and the air purge button used to allow the filter to fill with beerThe flow that can be seen coming from the red post that is connected to the yellow OUT disconnect is sanitiser being purged from the filter, generally about 100ml is sufficient for purgingFollowing purging the yellow OUT disconnect is fixed to the Kegs OUT post to allow filling of the keg through the kegs delivery tube

Beer being transferred under pressure from the Fermzilla via the filter into the kegs OUT post

As the keg fills it forces Co2 from the bottom of the keg through the 'Jumper' tube into the next awaiting keg

Use the volume calibration gauge to calculate the volume of beer that has been placed into the keg

From 58 litres, allow 1 litre for the filter = 57, less 19 = 38 first keg full, less 19 = 19 plus the filter volume of 1 litre will leave 1 litre of residual remaining

When the dip tube reaches the residual, as the residual is under pressure it is a firm surface for the pick up to lay lay on and does not cause emulsification of the beer and the residual

When all the beer has been taken into the dip tube only Co2 will enter the dip tube, not the residual, you can watch as the beer in the filter is replaced with Co2 then the outlet of the filter to the keg. Now is the time to disconnect the filters outlet to the keg

CHEERS!

www.ingramcontent.com/pod-product-compliance
Lightning Source LLC
Chambersburg PA
CBHW072053290426
44110CB00014B/1661